COLD FIRE

COLD FIRE

Verónica Zondek

Translated from the Spanish
by Katherine Silver

WORLD POETRY BOOKS

Originally published as *Fuego Frío*
(Santiago, Chile: LOM Ediciones, 2016)

This book is made possible with support from the
Stavros Niarchos Foundation.

Acknowledgement is made to the editors of *New Poetry in
Translation*, in which previous versions of "2" and "4" appeared.

First Edition, First Printing, 2022
ISBN 978-1-954218-98-7

World Poetry Books
New York, NY / Storrs, CT
www.worldpoetrybooks.com

Distributed by SPD/Small Press Distribution
Berkeley, CA
www.spdbooks.org

Library of Congress Control Number: 2022931556

Cover design by Boja
Typesetting by Alexandra Houdeshell & Don't Look Now
Printed in the USA by McNaughton & Gunn

UCONN
HUMANITIES INSTITUTE

This book is dedicated to my husband, Menashe; my sons: Assaf, Michael, and Daniel; my daughter, Tamara; and the sweet and eager eyes of Rafael, Manuel, Raiza, and Luciana: my grandchildren.

The tiny bones of tiny mice, of tiny birds more fragile than owls, of lizards, confirm what is already known: that life is always nourished by life and therefore it endures.

— Gustavo Boldrini, *Longotoma, Fragmentos de una novela imposible* (Fragments of an impossible novel), Ediciones Kultrún, 2016

1

It swoops
   swoops through
in a swoop uproots
            threads eyes
            sees expulsions
and flutters
      flutters
      flutters out times of trawling.

It pounds
   pounds the body into demented wings
   unleashes rain
               flaming torrents
               thunder
and sunders
   sunders the soul
nothing but it
            a belly dance
            a sentient spark.
Then it returns
            returns
            departs
            twists
            snags
            thunders at the peak with savage wing
and its rage
      its violet rage
is what stirs and burdens the air
with feet of lead.

Silence.

A silence falls
and the opalines fly in vain.

Caws
a bird caws.
It screeches
it sings its howl
and covers
                              with a warm-blooded hand
one breast of sky
one now calm
one now firebelching
as if it were merely a salve
                      a hit of crack
in tales of turmoil that burn/ inflame/ incinerate
these
the dark corridors of the sidereal proverb.
Neither fresh nor original.   Present.

A new instance of demented wing.

A maelstrom of fiery soul.

A mystery of crackling breath.

An *ay!*
          and it is brave.

Sweet, they say, is the company
                    the snores
                    the certain precipice of sky or
                        open sea
                    the punishment of the rod or the
                        prize to time passing
                    the dance of cold fire

uuuugh!...   and in something
in the littlest something

to find meaning.
Abyss
cliffs
desert sands
shelters open to the winging of the wind
                            of this anima
who
not achieving a name
possesses neither word nor cadence
yet
kicks up muffled madness
or
reposes in me
because
if I were ever someone
by now
I am but one of nothing

in the thick of pastures
and in thickwinds

trapped.

2

Now I need to talk about this listing/ rotting house/ its injured/ infirm/ wasted crumbs/ keeling till kneeling/ kissed to death by a fine/ pale/ mute finger/ red with green passion/ there/ among cold and exposed skeletons/ away from/ without/ regress.

Memory/ memory of what was once your house/ the forsaking of your house/ the whistling that runs through it/ that tears it apart/ breaks its panes/ sucks its sap/ only to leave it like this/ to forsake it as man/ now weary/ from one step to another/ the matter not other/ whatever.

Now you yield/ you depart/ you omit the mirror that dangles from quicksilver/ the blurred image/ suspended/ and you leave behind the table/ its oilcloth/ the plastic-hued flowers/ the toilet/ your chair of habit/ the hides drying in the wind/ ferrets by now a plague (how stupid/ look at the beast set free and left there to sing/) and the usual wind/ the never-never of a royal fairy tale/ there/ sniffing/ corroding at will/ as the ferret labors/ to balance us out/ natural.

Yes/ you depart/ you walk/ a few meters more/ a few meters less/ in the now already desert/ in the former musical forest/ and you begin/ you build again/ the same house but not/ same posts/ same planks/ same roof.

Illusion.

But between you and me/ no future other than/ a
new exodus/ neglect/ because the wind won't stop/
won't let you forget/ and returns/ returns with your
departure/ with your no resistance/ because you only
seek/ want/ wish/ wish to prosper/ prosper somehow/
no matter the sweat/ the tears/ the labor pains/ with
nothing/ to give and to take/ breath/ to dance and
to kill/ whistlings/ songs to life/ that one/ the one
that remains/ there beyond the passing bluster/
the vast skies/ the eternal boat/ the marketplace of
shipwrecks/ the bluish/ white/ gray/ dark failure/ and
yes/ yes gentlemen/ also the bird/ the trill/ the shrill/
yes/ all surrounded by howls/ by a heartbreaking owl/
he/ chest piercer/ caustic/ quiets/ because to breathe
is nothing/ and the windgust enshrouds/ imprisons/
silences/ silences speech/ the words in surplus/ and
pares us down/ binds us/ fences us in/ for the sake of
it/ for the sake of saying:

> you are... darling
> you are.

> But who hears your show/ your hoe?

> Your mother, darling/ your mother.

3

Now I walk/ I walk backward/ as if to unravel the traveled/ and all to know that what I caught sight of/ I saw:

Planks in the wind/ ashes/ tongueless flames/ they/ the usual suspects/ the blazing ones/ that reach into the pip/ the flayed bone/ the blind wit/ the stunned eyes/ and they/ those breezes that hang from a thread/ those gloves that don't graze against speech/ don't touch/ don't touch the blushing pastures/ the wounding rocks/ the ghost forests/ the voids of soul/ the voids of laughter/ the mute and the cracks left to soak.

Those/ the ones that sleep in their ink.

Yesterday/ only yesterday/ you were strutting your stuff. Today/ today you blink at me with your gaze/ you upend my pygmied wisdoms/ even though/ no/ you know nothing of names/ or houses/ or decorated windows.
No/ not of songs/ or dreams/ or fruits.
No
not of color braided into long tresses of affection.

I know only that you illuminate
                    embellish
                    burn longing
                         avarice/ covenant
and leave nothing but

a target   a white   white   very white target.

Because the Toothless Hag lurks unflagging/ and silence reigns/ and stages death/ and betrays life/ the random tune/ the heartbeat.
Now/ now she groans/ groans through herbaceous thunderclaps/ through wild flurries/ and it's that/ the scent of wet meat/ that seeps in slowly/ sleeps/ settles into your nails/

and

remains.

4

I climb the hill/ I see the lake/ and in the lake the mountains/ the dead trunks/ the living and tongueless tale/ the extinguished dream/ the clouds that pass/ and sing/ and boast/ and cry.

Fog/ blurred horizon/ scattered light/ time/ departed forest/ presence and absence in water/ because the world is other/ always an other/ a fragment of your evil/ or elusive beauty/ and I/ confronting your picture held in the face of the lake/ no longer know/ or will know/ who is the hooded one in charge/ what does he do or undo/ and why.

The wind drifts down
and is only absence
                  sea urchin sprouted from roving skin
as if without wanting
it has grasped uncompromising the tremulous
  gauge of the world.

And this that I am in the grasslands/ on the steppes shrouded in groaning whistles/ gallops/ now gallops/ and penetrates the left lobe/ and nestles into the belly/ and freezes movement/ and warns us/ and measures us/ and with violence

lowers us
lowers us to the source
there
where everything is but watery and fallow darkness
and the elements
are nothing but a distant presence.

Why so drawn to the wind?

Where?

Where does it store its wings?

When does it sleep?

Where will it go to die?

Why does it twist its neck?

Why does it lift the condor and lower her gently?

Where does it vanish?

No/ no way in hell/ because it blows fierce/ transfixes/
its stench transfixes/ its gasping inside my head/ its
shudder/ its shudder shuddering my guts/ eating me
up from inside/ torching me/ igniting the account of
the nobody that I am/ in other words/ straw/ straw
blown by breaths so huge/ so far from the eternal/ so
frigid/ so capricious/ so/ so fickle/ so/ until it breaks
the odd skeleton/ the small bones that pant/ that
beast-like bully/ and the uncontrollable stampede/
that one/ the one that sweeps through pygmy and
gasping trees/ the one without air to grow/ the one
that scours hillsides/ wuthering heights/ and gallops/
trots/ advances/ lifts seeds/ scatters them/ exiles them/
takes their homes/ their roofs away/ and shifts their
sands/ and destroys the sprouts/ and hardens/
hardens their snowy faces.

What beast?
What beast is that magnificent windgust that blows
upstream/ that climbs the heavens/ that moves clouds
to collapse over drought?

Meek burns the light through so much fog.

Meek is the cry of the forsaken bones.

Meek is the soul that watches and is flayed.

And on the horizon

a feeble/ wild light/ gallops/ gallops knowingly and displays its reins/ and batters/ batters without pity or pledges.

Now it closes the stars the ancient poem intoned/ and just imagine/ imagine it arriving to soak our drought/ to sprout it/ and sweet are the tears that fall from on high/ that pour down/ that fatten the grass/ an offering/ what/ which

that
what beasts and men chew/ of course/ more beasts than men............ yes............. to continue/ continue singing/ singing/ s ing   ing............

because strictly speaking/ they say/ they are only beasts/ beasts for men enswirled by wind/ by wind wind/ with its body so fragile/ my body/ and both so tied to/ so spun into memory/ into thought/ into love.

Why does the wind descend with its load of flames
that devours everything?

Look/ look how the lamb/ the huemul/ the puma run.
Look how the hillside is painted and howls red/ how
the woody bodies of the titans fall/ how water and
wind scar them...

What to do with so many spines turned away from the wind?

Who saw?

Who reports?

Might the condor be a floating witness in the windgusts?
Might it truly escape the iridescent tongues of evil?
Might it tell what it saw to the still intact mountainsides?
                    To the north that strengthens
                         and whistles and bites the ear?
                    To the vain man who never
                         learns his lesson?
                    To the scattered skeletons who
                        try to return to the earth?

Now

now the craven wind lights up the other hillside/ and
the dance descends/ and snow falls/ and the ferocious
tongue of the vermillion wolf covers everything/
and it goes astray once more/ and skitters along the
ground/ and grasps/ because no/ there is no bulwark
strong enough/ to withstand the stomping/ the blow
of blows/ the blow that never relents/ the blow.

Now

now comes the merriment/ and the warbling/ the
greening buds/ the nests and animal births.

And look!

It brings north and warmth of sun at once/ and
livens up the cueca/ and lifts the heads of fire/ and
dances it long/ and carved the wooden lizards fall/
their enormous heads

.... and they populate/ populate the vast lands.

Now the cloud appears and arrives encumbered/ with the shriek of lapwings.

Yes/ now the cloud appears and arrives wet/ and covers the mountain/ and descends/ and darkens/ and is blown forward/ and falls/ topples/ spills over the hillside/ and snow happens on the peak/ and the wind comes and blows on it/ tending it in flight/ and of course/ you can't/ you can't begin to imagine what that is/ you don't know how beautiful/ and it blows you from behind/ and the quill whirls/ and falls/ and rolls/ and fills the river below/ and the wind comes/ and draws white fleece/ and look/ now it cries/ bleats/ bleats with hunger/ without grass/ without woods/ without brushland.

Alone/ very much alone/ a little girl climbs/ shouts/ dwells on the rocky peak/ and queasy with colossal hunger/ she strums tunefully the open air of the sky/ and watches/ watches only watching/ until she buries her eyes into the settled ash/ into gray and white reality.

The wind is a king with a long and handsome tail.

The wind is lord and master of this territory.

The wind is great and does not have enough time.

The wind and the condor/ immensity.

All so alone/ so orphaned/ so exposed...

What is to be done?

You who are always here and see everything in this chatty humus/ be it my body or your body or our body/ and may all quiet forever/ may the lamb quiet/ and the cow/ the mare

and also

the condor/ the huemul/ the man/ the goat/ the lapwing/ the black-faced ibis/ and may the windgust reign supreme and its dangling wings/ that push the water/ that push the clouds/ that push the rain/ and erode the stones/ and erode the mount...

Who's watching now?

The fish that slips through the water?

The fish the man already caught?

The mañío tree that stubbornly endured?

The lenga/ the ñire/ the coigüe/ the laurel?

Then tell me what/ what will become of those dead bodies/ dead and black/ erect/ proud/ natural/ the in situ memorials/ for the pure pain of having been/ the pain of torsos/ the petty maiming/ and the naked boastful shout/ and the nobody listening/ because there is no ear anymore/ no eyelash/ no brow/ and only souls remain/ souls blackened and standing/ blackened and prone/ all asleep forever/ beheaded/ their guts exposed to rot/ love ready for matter/ amid winds that vanquish the grass and winds that bring the water down from the sky.

And
and now I think
that soon the time will come to dig the graves/ and the wind will be the gravedigger/ and it will bring seeds from far away/ and it will bring water/ earth and verses to adorn the dead/ bellies so wordy with sagas/ hands so playing the whistles of yore/ so covering the roads the wheel once rode on/ so swinging the bridges...

Who would have said so.../ who... who would have even thought so...

So now tell me if you are able to see your they/ your so tender and lush/ your children/ your loved ones...

Will they be the trace and path of your steps?
Will they carry the seed that will populate the
   barren ground?

I doubt/ I stammer.
It's just that
it's just that I glimpse their bended heads I say/ their
full torsos/ and though I know they do not desire/ do
not desire more golden tongues descending the slope
hand in hand with the wind/ do not want it/ I cannot
help but catch a glimpse/ a glimpse of their devout
knees poised like butterflies before you/ and I see/
right there I see/ how they make an effort/ how they
caress the idea of initiating novices/ tender sprouts/
sparks/ thirsty daughters/ all tattooed with the curse
of fire/ and I sense the coming of the forge/ how
they cannot fail to forge descendents/ mute beings
shrouded in windgusts/ for they did not fall when
blaze and heat/ and now they seem grateful/ because
dazzled they sing to the sun/ lift their legs/ their so
thin/ over any even black body in the river/ only
water this torrent/ aswirl at its vanishing points/
seething/ a crush of corpses where to rest the wing...

Look.

Observe your wounded/ lacerated body/ festered by
unruly wind.

Look.

Look how it slides unimpeded down the barren/ how down the trunkless immensity/ how down bald hillsides/ how through black skies/ lonely and cacique skies/ how/ how it gnaws/ how it gnaws at your body and before/ at your open tatters/ at your thirsty daughters/ at their mouths parched by so much wind/ and watch/ watch how it cries a torrential cry/ with tears once lost under the mutilated trunks/ and how it sprouts in wellheads everywhere/ and how it cascades descending/ how it uses its lost vision/ how it watches for atrocities/ senseless profit/ the beast that we are.

Who will stop it now?

Who will catch it and turn it into melody?

Who will comb the deepgreens/ a weave that clings with nails to Spanish moss?

Say it.

Say something more than the whistle that breaks my heart/ that breaks my rock/ that breaks my earth/ that bends my living bodies/ that pushes my threads/ that tans the hides/ the faces/ thought.

Because it tans the eye I tell you/ steals its water/ bedecks it with a smile/ leaves it naked/ rushing/ there/ sated/ swimming through the reeds/ building

its worlds/ undoing irascible/ irredeemable/ estates/
yes/ among so much and varied splendor.

Look/ look at its swollen gut/ look at the heights it
reaches...

That's how/ that's how it gives itself away.

That's how it sniffs out its prey, my dear:

that's how/ not otherwise:

all is silence and inhabits the icy gust and the
    wailing.

Look.

Look at the fleecy clouds in the sky/ the black ones
and the white.

Look.

Look how they travel together with speed and fury/
how they poke the watery ones with their spurs.

I'm telling you/ no/ they don't look/ they don't see/ there are no people/ there are no dogs/ there are no sheep/ there are no garments hanging their cleanliness out to dry/ only pyres of piled bodies/ their guilt hanging off them/ hanging in case there was sin/ because who/ who can counter the law if not them/ those who go to church/ those who are forgiven

a coin here

                                        a coin there

coins/ coins/ coins

and so/ which sin/ which one so great it weaves the trunks together/ gathers the corpses across ravaged pampas/ amassing them black/ blackened with time/ blackened with oblivion...

And before?

Just forest/ jungle/ humid/ dense jungle/ thriving in
meat/ in beats/ in passion...

And now...?

Now pyres/ pyres prepared for decay/ for the flames.

A wind/ a wind that opens the womb/ a wind that shakes the land/ that sprouts tenderness/ that squanders heat and swallows/ swallows the pain of men.

But no/ it doesn't come/ it doesn't grope/ it seems to be only when it kneads life/ when seedlings bloom/ and everything/ everything returns/ returns and begins again.

What is to be done?

The wind carries me off/ carries us off/ us up/ sings us from inside/ sings us from outside.
The bird boosts/ raises/ rinses/ recites its wings/ considers us/ peals its eye/ looks at my feet/ my fingers/ the ones embedded/ because the humus is alive/ it boils/ it warms/ it summons/ ay/ what can I do/ what can I do if to me the wind/ to us the wind/ and the rock loosened/ scarred/ lets out a shout/ tells the tale/ and says:

Who?

Who are you?

What are you doing on this ground?

What did you do?

....
... So
it happens that the world happens/ and keeps happening like someone turning the pages of a book.

Neither doubt nor discussion/ silence.
Silence and incident.
Wind/ wind that passes through/ that raises duststorms/ that erases all traces.

Wind that takes
        that brings
        that drops water
                timeless
                        perplexed
                                harmless
in the well-known perfection that/ of course/ preceded
the miserable arrival of/ of course/ the knight errant

and voracious.../ now mounted on his beast.

Can woman/ man/ be quiet and receive?
Can woman/ man/ refrain from sullying
the airborne muteness of the pampas?
                        Of the eternal forest?
                        Of the ice?
Can they?
Can silence be the only actor in the vastness?

And farther away/ there where the lunar craters
establish a known address/ can it/ can the storm
wrap thunder in the arena of the lone one?
And..................... how many are there?
How many are the dreams?
                The buried who retreat?
How many who nod off under the dust?
                        Under the immutable light?

How many?
How many who breathe under the red ash?
How many under the bluegreen flame?

Who?
Who is able to make them shine?
Who to make them speak?

Well, I say nobody/ nobody is known to have managed.

Here/ here words aren't woven.

The wind whistles and groans and roars/ and all flies
and is guttural.

A dark hand this gale.
An albino hand of absent mouths/ silence.

Silence.

Glaucous silence here to stay.

5

Fragments.

The earth a fragment/ the wind a fragment/ the birds/ the labor/ the mountains/ the seas.

The bones a fragment/ the horse skulls/ the hides/ the lust for power.

Rough texture a fragment/ the written word/ the small print between rocks/ sculpted silences for the deceased/ the dead ones/ the vanished greenery/ those that flutter among the living/ pasturelands in flames/ those that burn/ that seal the track with a branding iron/ trunks that shout/ that speak/ that corrode a thought.

A fragment that points with a hand/ with an axe/ an ember/ a large candle on the bald prairie/ in the spooked/ furious ledger/ trapped between winds and false bluster/ in the waters of whatever's there.

A fragment of a whole/ of a nothing/ we breathe now/ we breathe tomorrow/ hmmm................../ memory is wearisome/ the finger is wise/ and today/ oblivion is lack of/ because the air is the wind/ transparency/ strife/ a small piece of something/ hmmm................../ and hangs/ hangs from those crosses the wind gave birth to/ a seed/ a being/ an illusion/ hmmm.................. of life/ of life today contained/ tomorrow nomadic/ but always and still between/ between betweens/ between the betweens of war forever more.

6

Take a look/ time is corrupt/ disrupts/ envelops the air in the cough of a wandering bull/ and charges and attacks and embraces lands/ men/ forests/ birds/ waters/ and of course/ punctures/ punctures this petrified silence/ into the asthmatic ayyayyays of today/ only highwaters/ friends of the wind/ aphonia in the very pith of natural death.

And what is to be done if the wind is wind/ and it pursues us/ ensues us/ scratches our defeated trunks/ the ripe ripening under the sun/ and pursues with choked splutters the fallen/ and the burned/ and the beaches/ and the darkness/ and...

runs/ runs/ runs a race outrunning the stormcloud/ and damn/ the heavens are so vast I no longer know/ because where/ where are they/ where do they go/ because I know/ I know that flies can't enter a closed mouth/ and that female ducks endure/ and so do she-herons/ condors/ ewes/ cows/ goats/ huemulas/ pheasants and hares/ and okay/ so do a few boys and men/ such grand girls and women/ and the houses/ and everything and everyone close their mouths/ so the wind won't enter/ won't attack/ so it won't flay us/ so it won't uproot us/ so it won't blow us away/ even if it does swoop up the leaves/ and make the solid waters flinch/ flinch/ and stoke the flames/ and scratch the peaks of the Andes.

Then the shout
the shout

the eeeeeeeeeeeeeee till I'm sick of it
because no
I don't want flight
no
I don't want fire
I don't want it climbing the haunches
mounted on the endless wind
I don't want it heating surfaces
burning vegetal/ fleshy/ pink skins
I don't want it dancing
I don't want it out of control in the middle of orgies
without pleasure/ or love/ or meat on the hot grill.
No/ I don't want the banality of it printing/ sealing/
caressing
that

the royal plan.

Yes.
The hands of others.
Banality of evil.

7

Look.
A skeleton lies naked on the pampas.

The hill sleeps and the dead man sleeps and asleep
  are the burned-out bodies.

Out in the world two ñire trees still chat like two
  old men.
Two babble on the butchered earth.
Cows/ mares/ goats
there
when the retreat of the waters.

We always bleed through our wounds.

Man or whale...

Death is black
and commands.

8

Honored skull
dear girl:
I write these words so that
you'll shelter grassblades in your gaping holes
     shelter wind that rocks your imaginary mane
          a little flower that sprouts your hollow eye
          and your ornament of past glories.
Ay!
Look how the mortal embrace of these eager dames presses
how they soak their fleshy bodies in colossal ocean depths.
Look at them/ look how they stand firm in the middle of
the stunned and sleeping landscape.

Life and death

eager
so eager

and nothing.

Maybe a cemetery
        a tiny dated house
        a floral scattering
says something
carries something

and nothing.
It blows/ sings/ rings.
It blows and groans.

It blows/ laughs/ breathes.
Life flickers its details between sunglares.
Hell landed smack in the middle of paradise
that one/ the one they painted to please us.
Now they sing the waters
                    their laments
                    their marbled affections

and nothing.

There's a wind that needs the earth to work.
There's an earth that needs the wind to sprout.
There's an earth that needs the wind and lends its
    ears to its need.
There's an earth that sustains us in spite of us.
There's a wind that speaks for us

and nothing.

Our hands remain
and know labor
and humble and titanic and toiling
they thread needles
wield hammers/ sickles
cradle children
        dark songs of assent
and with fire establish the word
the one that slips/ the one that numbs thought on
the tongue
the one that carries/ transports/ invents us anew.

9

Now the flame advances/ and the smell of burning spreads/ of scorched bodies/ of smoked forests/ of roasted wild fruits/ of charred plumage/ of golden sheepskins/ of all sorts and scents of meat/ and rot flinches/ and life grows complicated/ fire lays waste/ slopes/ pasturelands weep/ and then/ then green spreads/ stretches/ with the entire length of its living body over the white and drunken pallet of memory.

Now it has been summoned/ called to judgment:

1st: The wind denounced
2nd: Tried in court
3rd: Convicted

And silence/ silence gentlemen./ We shall announce the verdict:

Guilty Mr. Wind./ Guilty./ You, sir, are guilty.

And why/ why don't you listen to what they are saying, Your Honor:

"It was our neighbor/ that arrogant ass/ that lover of fire/ the one who failed to see/ who ignored me/ forgot my presence/ the snow/ the birds/ and with ardor he cleansed his land/ he said he'd bring animals and didn't/ he said I'll burn only this small patch and couldn't/ and he burned/ forever burned the forests/ the now dead/ those prone and in heaps/ to the delight of your eyes and to your eternal sadness."

"I'll tell you/ Your Honor/ the real reason sir/ even if you don't believe it."

Where the mother?
        The son?
        The daughter?
Where the tree?
        The song?
        The bread?

The wind hisses/ ignores us/ stabs us/ pushes us aside/ leaves us to eat with our eyes.

The Song withers/ hushes/ is engulfed by the prairie/ the pasture/ the cows/ the equines/ the hens and their roosters/ the sheep.
The Swan's Song no longer/ no longer.
Only Sirens' Songs/ their presence that meanders through the mountains in silence when the waters eject them.

Everything is lost among the lingual/ bloody/ reddened glints/ feverish with death/ displaced/ into twisted fumes unending/ into lost and scrambled pathways/ into the bonfire.

Pathways/ pathways of nothingness.
Until further notice sir.
Over there sir/ there/ there beyond the mouth/ of a possible repentant someone/ neutered/ besieged/ speechless/ cut short.

Everything is.
Everything is understood among matter and matter
    and matter.
Life pulsates in every corner.

It depends on you said the rabbit
and changed burrows/ and pricked up her ears/ and
spoke:

Let there be light.
My name names.
My name is fertility.

It depends on you said the rabbit
and changed burrows/ and pricked up her ears/ and
spoke:

Let there be light.
My name names/ a, b, c, d, e...

Guardian of time

look how you drop your elements/ your weight/ your drawing/ your handwriting/ and how like a supplicant you rush from hand to hand/ from body to body/ until you are left without clothing/ among voices and silences already muted by long-ago fires.

And yes/ there is hunger/ hunger of ancient density/ the kind that cannot be sated/ that eats the living forest/ that meanders the ominous cliffs/ that dreams the sea that in the beyond/ the waves/ the wind/ the sky/ the rainbow unfurled/ the full-throated man/ his song/ the words and their gales/ the timbers/ the birds of prey.

The lion is famished and descends the mountain...

Man is famished and accumulates...

11

Rain falls.

A voice falls into a vacuum.
Night falls into the dark.
Silence falls.
Light falls over the backbones of the cold stones.
Wings fall to the cliff.
Water falls.
Water

falls.

12

Now at last/ only silence and green bones.
Creakings/ open hillsides/ slopes for the stream's
song/ peaks for raptors/ footsteps of a vacant man/ ...

What did I do?
Why so much hunger?
Where does this barb in the wire lead...?

13

Tombs of silence in an annotated landscape.
Tombs of earth
      of forests
      of glances exchanged.

Tombs.
Banishment.
Witnesses passing............ from the shores we leave
and passengers witnessing............ from the ship
  that carries us across.
No rowers I say/ no rudder for the crossing.

And this earth
           its measured time
and the names/ the light/ the cold wind
fall
fall falling headlong
like before in Canto 11 of this poem
fall
fall falling headlong
for if the bloody grass loses its balance
plain as day it will collapse
and crash flat down
into the many and any violet tongues hugging the
  trunks
in order to see/ discern an upright dance
a stable tremor of wings
and arms/ octopuses/ vanes
and men/ and women/ and children
all of them carried from where they were born to the
other side/ the other shore

left
there
barechested
empty.

Silence.

Again a silence happens
as now and now and now as before I mentioned
and never
never will I tire of mentioning
because this loaded silence
loaded with lost/ squandered/ sold gold
wraps us in its melody
strips bare our chests
opens our souls before it falls to our feet
to crackle and speak
and give thanks to life and its goddamn wind
and be left with meaning and knowledge
well-placed/ a bit dirty
but with wings of such tender filigrees
that I no longer know and never will.

14

Wounded I go forth/ cutting branches/ kicking stones/ reading stones/ amassing stones/ and I observe/ observe that pink and placid huemul/ while the cold wolf/ the scythe that sits in wait blows/ blows/ blows/ and I tremble/ tremble/ tremble in the silence of your cursed trawls/ and I sing/ sing/ sing quietly/ adrift/ solitary ship/ bird of mutilated wings/ quill that writes/ a word alone/ alone

in the wind.

15

Better I had not seen
        not looked at the affliction
        not touched the faded ash
all that the fire of fires lulled on the ground.
Better.
But I witnessed/ I touched them/ the galloping quavers
on the wind with the unfurled skin of my index finger/
and hence they turned to dust in my eye.
And it is now
now that everything is black and yellow
and the blue only floats suspended
and places its silence in nothingness
in what was
even if it doesn't matter one damn bit
because the wind returns
returns and churns
and the seed descends/ descends and settles
and multiplies/ among transparent breaths it multi-
plies/ and buries/ buried among greens/ and browns/
and bloody ambers
and sprouts/ sprouts the nourishing placenta
because this abortion does not stop
even though no
nobody
not my mother
not my children
not I
not you
wants it.

If only to save its cheerful face
                its party dress
                its sunny trills
                its lit-up longing
amid so much unstoppable greed.

Many arms unnamed and unknown
lie muffled and occult in the bulging pockets
of the faces they offend/ freeze/ dirty their hands
and
wear them down/ and wither their *sube a nacer conmigo,
hermano.*

An inept silence moves in at the wrong time.

A zeal erodes the treachery.

These outposts nurture the gift of bounty
and therein dances the deep meaning of the precious.
There's a fount tangled up with my limbs
all flooded with thunder and tumbling skies.
There's a windgust with an implacable lash.
There's a memory and it is only and it is sometimes
sometimes it resolves something
some fantasy illuminated by green and turbulent skies
and
chills/ solitudes/ famines in the inlands or out at sea.
Inevitable companions
                in the midst
                        of...
Can we manage with and beyond falseness?

Mute misery among us and also a deaf ear:

because here the time has come/ the plain/ the plainness.
Yes.
Yes friends/ comrades/ citizens/ brothers
have no doubt
here are the signs/ the clues/ the numbers all.
Here are the deeds and what has not been done.

Yes
either we hit the cat on the head or depart this world
with thickened eyes.

16

It comes/ here it comes.

It is.

It is

it is a wind of death/ a wind that sneaks in/ that enters/ that through the window enters/ that through the door leaves/ and through the door uproots/ uproots life/ life that flees/ the void of emptiness/ and falls/ falls to the renovated earth/ independent of you/ stubborn regrowth/ radiance woven into kisses/ into bones/ into beds that cradle the other/ hope/ conception/ bodies that do not slacken/ hands that set to work/ that baste as best they can/ that desire/ that try and try again/ that embroider the void/ that cover it with stitches/ and enter/ enter the eye of the storm/ enter as they enter/ caressing it/ adopting it skyblue/ dead/ alive/ among all the hanging garments/ the white ones/ the ones that sway in the air/ so it will remember/ so it will catch lost sorrows/ so it will name them/ so it will leave them in flames.

17

The grass sways/ the blades bend/ the saps and their old age weep.

The pudú flees in terror.

Birds take flight/ flap their wings/ scream/ whistle/ and sing the mortuary rites of the chirping carmine tongues.

Now fire lays siege/ melts barbs/ fences/ and invokes/ invokes deeply the ancient blush/ and thunder descends/ and water falls/ and the deranged one blows.

Then snow arrives/ and falls/ falls/ falls mutely/ and covers/ covers albino the fever of the earth/ its delirium/ its bewildered ants/ its critters/ its ardor/ its ground/ and buried is malice/ the red lie/ and quiets/ quiets winter/ and the now faded remains grow quiet/ and the sun rests for a while/ and hides out of sight/ and/ and/ and/ and gone are the seasons/ dormant under smoke/ and/ and/ and/ and gone are birds who sing/ and/ and gone is the break of dawn/ as if eternity had sat down forever at the table/ a parishioner upon defiled/ sullied ground/ wrapped in ash paper

and fog.

For whom the offering?

Silence.

Stealth and stillness.

It's time
it's time to fatten this silence in the mud home
    earth gave us.

Maybe it's time to turn the page because like in a
fairy tale and although no one ever really knew
how/ you should know that the sun returned/ and it
returned because it wanted to get married and have
lots of sons and daughters and make bricks/ bricks
for the castle walls/ to live among the sparkles/ be
a little bit happy/ even if everything had to begin
anew/ without Adam/ without Eve/ without the
serpent/ without gods to sing the news.

And it did return/ it returned from afar/ touched the
horizon with its sword/ light rose along spider webs
woven into the shadows/ melted the ice/ the snow/
the cold/ and then we saw the spluttering of fierce
tongues/ their bashful dances/ skirts raised/ ankles
displayed/ its advance/ till it was nothing but gold/
red gold in the blue of the elements/ earthly hell/
absence of humans/ of upright trunks just barely
clinging to/ of scorched leaves/ of roasted and
appetizing birds.

And despite it all/ the dance.

The dance must continue/ vomit up its ardor/ pound
its hooves/ as if the sentence were not yet written/
nor the letter/ nor the book/ nor the good intentions

that would say I stay/ I will return/ it is I/ the pulse
of the surroundings/ in suspension/ yes

but no

I don't lie down on the broken earth.

18

Do you think a skeleton sees?

Will the hummingbird's beating heart nest within it?

Will it hear the song of a black-faced ibis in heat?

Because there are skeletons/ skeletons of the blood
and skeletons of the sap.
Skeletons/ skeletons everywhere/ dead forests/ dead
forests everywhere.
Houses/ deserted houses/ fine brocades/ pearly lace/
tablecloths spread over grassland/ naked lunches/
men without flesh/ shadows/ fantasy shadows/
fantasy forests draped in graying waters/ in winds
of names/ of gods/ of times from who knows when.
Landscape/ landscape that no
no
no longer is possible to recognize/ to roam/ to reread.
Yet/ it gets easier to guess tomorrow/ to listen to the
bird/ to life/ and to know that with skill everything
quiets/ to know that it comes/ that it comes/ that it
comes filled with seeds/ as the wind before/ the wind/
the wind that embraces the landscape
and that tree.................... a tree/ a tree/
one tree added to another tree/ a forest/ a jungle/ a
starting point/ a green/ all lost among the shaded
blues and bloody reds of the hidden gorges
and yes
we
one eye.................... one eye to read the easy grace

a splendor
of

don't touch me
or
touch me softly
sing to me
use me in powerful rivers
       in seas of castaways
just don't try to sweeten me up among so many
  deranged tongues.
Now
now comes the elusive shadow/ the one that slips
through fingers
yes
the one stripped of humors
           of sleeping plants
and then
I forget/ you should too
and your trapdoor
open
   to the peephole of desire
   to the kinetic necessity spilled and everywhere
that
that irresistible attraction
that reproduction/ that onomatopoeia/ that one
specimen
that one plus another one and yet another one
that now adds up to specimens three

vision
mathematics of bodies wrapped in passion

> their perfume
> their supremacy
> their...

Ay/ yes
embryonic
we touch warm blood/ viscous sap
in times of ingratitude and other reckless epithets
because then
though sad/ withdrawn/ fruitful
it's here/ it appears/ it appears/ a new flight appears/
a beaten path that carries us down to warm ground/
a walking through the heavens/ a touching of rivers/
a celebration of the fertile/ of all that comes to us
by chance and we can embrace/ chew/ admire/ love/
surprise.

19

Now I see your wild gestures/ your jaw/ your smile.
I see your teeth/ your defeated trunk/ your gnawed
body/ also the very impotent in the face of time/
the very licked by tongues of silence/ and the very
odorless...........................

Clear.
Clear as water.

They no longer climb.
They no longer dance.

Gone the windgust/ and also the shadow of the bodies.

Gone the carnal/ and also the hot master of time.

In this pit dwells death.
Death dwells in the middle of blackness.
Death dwells in the angel of the well.
Death is a great yawn that breaks out everywhere.

The brigand cries.
Laughs.

20

To dwell in a blue forest.

To dwell in a whitened time that fades desire.

To dwell in a profound installation of oblivion.

To dwell in a verb of personal responsibility.

To dwell in a verb of generous embrace.

To say no
there is no law that restrains enormity
nor thought that fully ripens it.

Listen!
May it never be said that man was not here!
May it never be said that here he did not roam!

                                    Roam?

Listen
listen to what matter says/ do not get distracted/ stay
still/ converse with it.
Do not give up.
Think.
Think that you are nothing but a train stop.
One.

One fleeting station.
Then:
love/ smile and cry/ sleep/ dream/ kiss with passion
stop/ look/ listen/ stop and let the silver fingers of the
windgust touch you/ and the golden fingers of the
cold fires/ for my letter on the page sleeps while it
waits for the slow roar of awakening/ devouring what
voracious tongues have left behind/ inhaling the tears
of the defeated/ sowing eyes far and wide/ for our duty
is to read/ and reread/ and pay heed/ even if we are
only blood/ and bone/ and dream/ in this long/ long
and slow bog.

Look!
Let it sprout unscathed!

Hence the airs/ the waters/ the insects from who
knows where/ or when...................................
may they say/ say/ murmur/ say/ say and whisper/

whisper into the ears of all the loan sharks circulating
through the imaginary streets of this landscape/
murmur/ murmur/ say/ say and whisper:

no more
no more rapacity without rhyme or reason.........

Look around.

Draw conclusions.

VERÓNICA ZONDEK is one of Chile's most renowned and prolific poets, translators, and editors. She has published many books of poetry, and has collaborated extensively with musicians, visual artists, photographers, dancers, and performance artists. She published a critical edition of the poetry of Nobel Prize-winning poet Gabriela Mistral. Her translations include the works of Gottfried Benn, Derek Walcott, June Jordan, Anne Carson, Emily Dickinson, Anne Sexton, and Gertrude Stein. She lives in Valdivia, Chile.

KATHERINE SILVER's most recent and forthcoming translations include works by María Sonia Cristoff, César Aira, Juan Carlos Onetti, and Julio Ramón Ribeyro (winner of the Premio Valle-Inclán 2020). She is the former director of the Banff International Literary Translation Centre (BILTC), and the author of *Echo Under Story*. She does volunteer interpreting for asylum seekers.

The text of *Cold Fire* is set in Sabon LT Pro.
Typesetting by Alexandra Houdeshell and Don't Look Now.
Cover design by Boja.
Printed and bound in Saline, Michigan
at McNaughton & Gunn.

WORLD POETRY BOOKS

Jean-Paul Auxeméry | *Selected Poems*
tr. Nathaniel Tarn

Maria Borio | *Transparencies*
tr. Danielle Pieratti

Jeannette L. Clariond | *Goddesses of Water*
tr. Samantha Schnee

Jacques Darras | *John Scotus Eriugena at Laon*
tr. Richard Sieburth

Jerzy Ficowski | *Everything I Don't Know*
tr. Jennifer Grotz & Piotr Sommer
PEN AWARD FOR POETRY IN TRANSLATION

Antonio Gamoneda | *Book of the Cold*
tr. Katherine M. Hedeen & Víctor Rodríguez Núñez

Phoebe Giannisi | *Homerica*
tr. Brian Sneeden

Nakedness Is My End: Poems from the Greek Anthology
tr. Edmund Keeley

Jazra Khaleed | *The Light That Burns Us*
ed. Karen Van Dyck; tr. Peter Constantine, Sarah McCann, Max Ritvo,
Angelos Sakkis, Josephine Simple, Brian Sneeden, & Karen Van Dyck

Maria Laina | *Hers*
tr. Karen Van Dyck

Maria Laina | *Rose Fear*
tr. Sarah McCann

Perrin Langda | *A Few Microseconds on Earth*
tr. Pauline Levy Valensi

Giovanni Pascoli | *Last Dream*
tr. Geoffrey Brock
RAIZISS/DE PALCHI TRANSLATION AWARD

Rainer Maria Rilke | *Where the Paths Do Not Go*
tr. Burton Pike

Elisabeth Rynell | *Night Talks*
tr. Rika Lesser

Ardengo Soffici | *Simultaneities & Lyric Chemisms*
tr. Olivia E. Sears

Ye Lijun | *My Mountain Country*
tr. Fiona Sze-Lorrain

Verónica Zondek | *Cold Fire*
tr. Katherine Silver